Book 1   Grade 1

The Graded Piano Player

Well-known tunes specially arranged by leading educationalists

FABER *ff* MUSIC

© 2016 by Faber Music Ltd
Bloomsbury House
74–77 Great Russell Street
London
WC1B 3DA

Music setting by MusicSet2000
Cover design by Chloë Alexander
Page design by Susan Clarke

Printed in England by Caligraving Ltd

ISBN10: 0-571-53940-8
EAN13: 978-0-571-53940-6

To buy Faber Music publications or to find out about the full range of titles available
please contact your local music retailer or Faber Music sales enquiries:
Faber Music Ltd, Burnt Mill, Elizabeth Way, Harlow CM20 2HX
Tel: +44 (0) 1279 82 89 82   Fax: 44 (0) 1279 82 89 83
sales@fabermusic.com   fabermusicstore.com

Contents

Hakuna Matata

from Walt Disney Pictures' *The Lion King*

Arranged by Christopher Hussey

Music by Elton John
Lyrics by Tim Rice

Auld Lang Syne

Arranged by Alan Bullard

Traditional

Can you feel the love tonight

from Walt Disney Pictures' *The Lion King*

Arranged by Christopher Hussey

Music by Elton John
Lyrics by Tim Rice

Close every door

from *Joseph and the Amazing Technicolor® Dreamcoat*

Arranged by Alan Bullard

Music by Andrew Lloyd Webber
Lyrics by Tim Rice

Summertime

from *Porgy and Bess*®

Arranged by Ned Bennett

Music and Lyrics by George Gershwin, Du Bose
and Dorothy Heyward and Ira Gershwin

All I want

Arranged by Alan Bullard

Words and Music by Mark Prendergast, James Flannigan,
Stephen Garrigan and Vincent May

I wan'na be like you (The monkey song)

from Walt Disney's *The Jungle Book*

Arranged by Alan Bullard

Words and Music by Richard M. Sherman and Robert B. Sherman

Brightly

Where is love?

from *Oliver*

Arranged by Christopher Hussey

Words and Music by Lionel Bart

Memory

from Cats

Arranged by Alan Bullard

Music by Andrew Lloyd Webber
Text by Trevor Nunn after T. S. Eliot

Deep river

Arranged by Ned Bennett

Traditional

Sunny afternoon

Arranged by Ned Bennett

Words and Music by Ray Davies